Opal Town

Rob Waring, *Series Editor*

HEINLE
CENGAGE Learning

Australia • Brazil • Japan • Korea • Mexico • Singapore • Spain • United Kingdom • United States

Words to Know

This story is set in Australia, in the town of Coober Pedy [kubər pidi], which is in the state of South Australia.

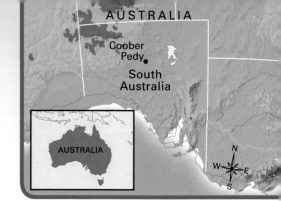

 The Beauty of Opals. Read the paragraph. Then match each word with the correct definition.

Opals are one of the most beautiful gems in the world because they tend to shine and sparkle in the light. They also can contain many different colors, including blue, green, and red, which change in intensity as light is reflected. Sometimes they're brighter in color; sometimes they're deeper. This makes opals a very popular precious stone for decorating jewelry and other items.

1. opal _____	**a.** shine brightly and reflect bits of light
2. gem _____	**b.** the degree or strength of something
3. sparkle _____	**c.** a stone with bright colors, often made into jewelry
4. intensity _____	**d.** a general term for valuable stones, usually cut into a shape
5. precious _____	**e.** extremely valuable because of price, importance, or lack of availability

sapphire

B **A Mining Town.** Read the paragraph. Use the basic form of the underlined words or phrases to complete the definitions.

This story is about one of the world's most important places to <u>mine</u> precious opals: Coober Pedy, Australia. Coober Pedy is located in an Australian wilderness area known as <u>the outback</u>. This part of Australia is very hot and dry, and the <u>landscape</u> is relatively flat and often treeless. Despite this, people from all over the world go to Cooper Pedy regularly to <u>stake a claim</u> and get some land. They come with a dream of getting rich by finding opals deep in the underground <u>tunnels</u> beneath the town.

1. the general features and characteristics of the land: _____

2. declare something for oneself: _____

3. take minerals or valuable materials out of the earth: _____

4. the areas of Australia that are far away from towns and cities: _____

5. a long, narrow, underground opening usually used for travel or moving things: _____

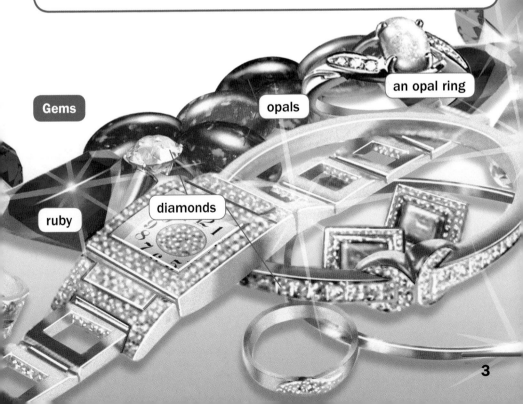

an opal ring

Gems

opals

diamonds

ruby

In the incredible heat of the Australian outback, the soil has been burned by the sun. The landscape doesn't look very welcoming, but beneath the dry surface, there are valuable treasures to be found. As one nears the town of Coober Pedy, South Australia, huge fields of small hills cover the land. They're made of the dirt that has been taken from the endless underground tunnels in the area. Here, deep under the earth, one can find men digging almost every hour of every day. They use huge machines to create large networks of holes under the ground. These men are digging for something that—if they find it—may make them rich and change their lives forever: opals.

Peter Rowe is one of several miners who have made Coober Pedy their home. After a tour of the mines, Rowe explains why he came to this town in the middle of the outback. For him, it's all about the money. He explains in his own words: "I came here to make a million dollars. I heard you could make a million dollars in Coober Pedy, and I [have] come to get my share of it!"

 CD 1, Track 07

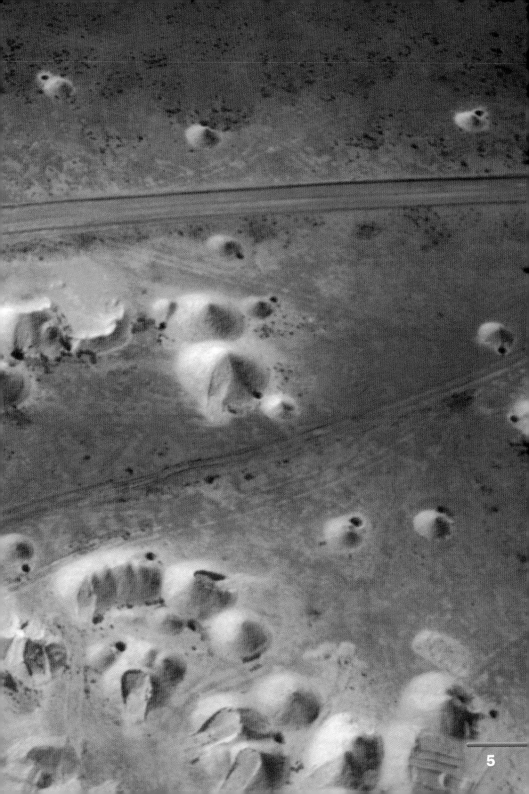

5

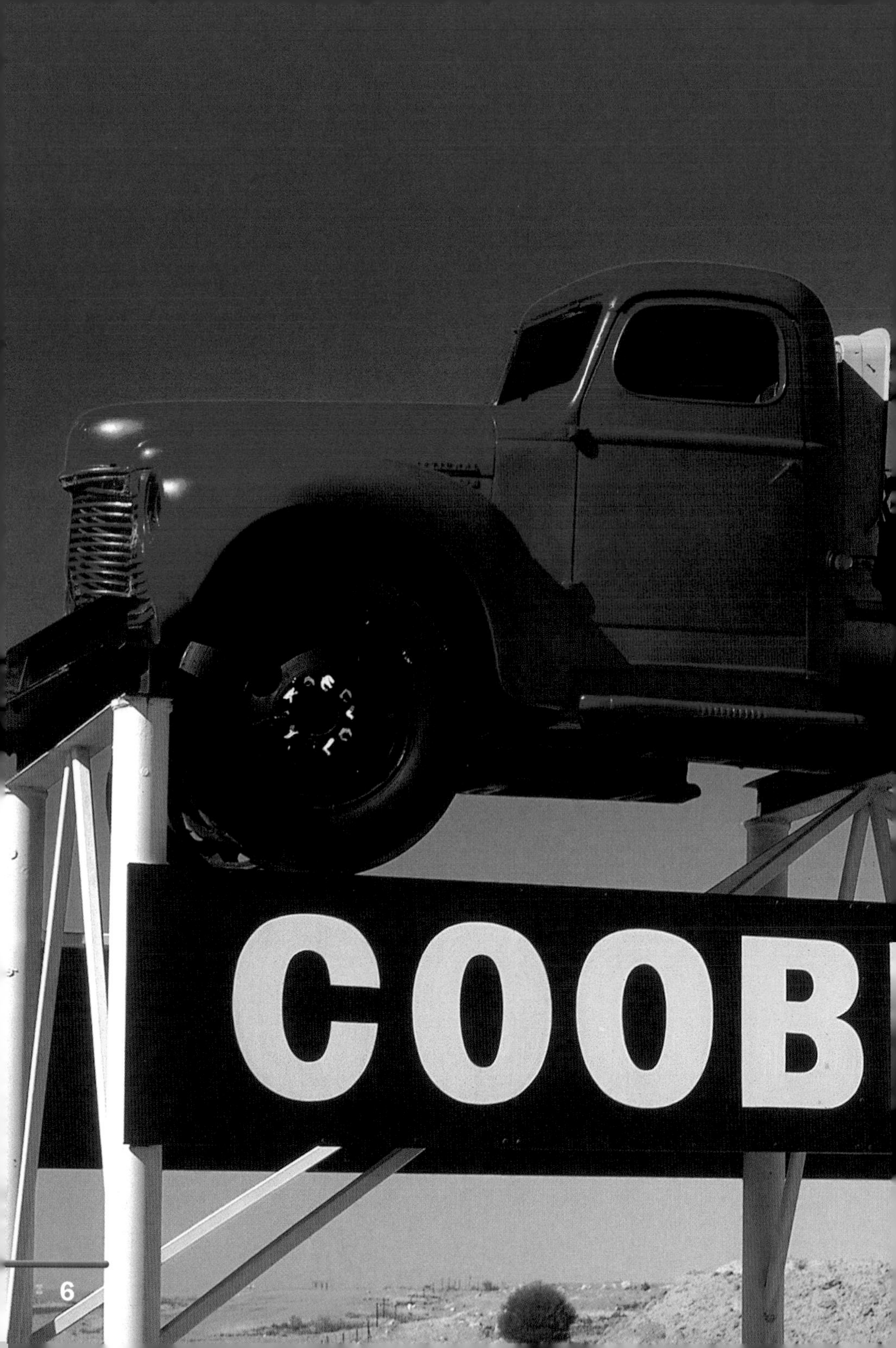
COOB

Rowe then offers an explanation of what the other miners are searching for. He knows that they want the one big precious gem that's going to be worth a great amount of money. "That is what they came here for," Rowe explains, "to find that **elusive**,[1] beautiful gem that just sort of **bounces out**[2] and says 'Hey, look at me!'"

If gems are what these miners are looking for, Coober Pedy is the right place to begin the search. Coober Pedy, a town of only about 3,000 people, is the 'opal capital' of Australia. Opals have always been the basis for the economy of the town and a main source of income for people living in and around it. In fact, opal mining is still the most important economic activity in the region. Ninety percent of the world's opals come from Australia, and the first ones on the continent were discovered in Coober Pedy in 1913.

---

[1]**elusive:** difficult to find
[2]**bounce out:** (*uncommon use*) stand out among other things

Today, people can find these beautiful gems at local shops in Coober Pedy, including one owned by opal merchant **Yanni Athanasiadis**.[3] This shop owner is an expert in opals who knows the most important contributor to their value. "Color," he says, and then repeats himself to emphasize the point quite simply, "What makes [an] opal is color."

There are several different types of opals, and crystal opals—the kind most often found in Coober Pedy—are very valuable. However, as with any type of opal, it is the variety and intensity of the color, or colors, that make it sparkle in the light. It's also the number of colors, or 'fires,' in the opal that make it particularly valuable. Rowe explains, "If you've got a piece of opal that [let's] say has just got blue color, [or] blue 'fire,' in it—that's all—its **monetary**[4] value is nowhere near as valuable as a piece of opal that has got red and blue for instance. But if it's got red, blue, orange, and green—wow! And they're rare."

---

[3]**Yanni Athanasiadis:** [yɑni ɑθənəsyɑdɪs, æθ]
[4]**monetary:** of or related to money

These days, finding these rare opals has been turned into as much of a science as the rock will allow. Small teams of miners stake claims to specific areas in which they would like to mine for opals. They carefully study the earth and choose places where the soil and stone come together in patterns which suggest that opals are there. Even so, it's extremely difficult to predict where the opals are located within the rock.

One such team of three men has been digging for a year and a half since their last significant opal discovery. That's 18 months without any luck. However, the soil in the area where they are digging now is showing signs that there may be opals nearby. The team believes that they are only a few feet away from a major find. They're really excited about it as they prepare to go underground. The men first check the soil in the mining area by hand and then carefully use their machines to continue digging. They can't risk making a mistake at this point!

Fact Check: True or false?

1. It's difficult to know where one is going to find valuable opals.

2. Shape is what makes an opal valuable.

3. The miners on page 10 haven't found a valuable opal in 18 years.

4. They now believe that they are close to finding valuable gems.

The mining team thinks they can tell where valuable opals are located by examining the soil, but is it science or experience that helps them find the opals? One of the team members, Neville Hyatt, feels that it's mainly due to what he's seen and done himself. "It's experience more than anything," he says. He then adds that there is no promise that the team will find opals—even in the area that looks hopeful. "[We can guess] that's normally where it is," he explains and then adds with a laugh, "But there are no rules. There [are] just sort of 'recommendations' if you like."

The problem with opal mining is that, in a town like Coober Pedy, almost everyone believes that he or she is about to find a **fortune**.[5] Unfortunately it doesn't happen often, but sometimes those dreams do come true. High-quality opals can bring huge amounts of money. The number of opals that can be cut from a **fist-sized**[6] piece of opal will sell for at least 300,000 Australian dollars—or maybe a lot more!

---

[5]**fortune:** a large amount of money
[6]**fist-sized:** the same approximate size as a person's hand with the fingers gripped tightly inward

According to Yanni Athanasiadis, the opal expert, there are a number of factors in the art of opal valuation. As he examines a few different opals, he explains the more important factors in the pricing of opals. "The pattern of the color, the thickness of the stone, the shape of the stone," he says, "[all of these things] will determine the last price that we put on the opal."

An opal's color is generally considered to be the most important factor in its value. However there is a reason for this high assignment of value: there are not a lot of opals that even have color. Ninety-five percent of all opals are colorless and therefore worthless. There are huge underground networks of tunnels in Coober Pedy that did not produce even a dollar's worth of opals. Many times the only thing the miners have to show after all of their hard work is just a big hole in the ground. However, there can be interesting benefits to even these big holes ...

The more creative people in the town of Coober Pedy have made these holes into homes. The climate conditions in the area around the town can be quite extreme. Temperatures can reach as high as 30 degrees Celsius in the daytime and drop down to single-number temperatures at night. The holes that have been made into homes, or 'cave **dwellings**',[7] are much easier to regulate in temperature than typical houses.

Hyatt and some of his mining partners actually live in these cave dwellings with their families. The team and their families have gathered in one of the dwellings to take some time to relax together. They need to be refreshed and ready before they start their big push to find opals in the promising area that they've found. They sit down to eat around a large table in a mining hole that's been turned into a dining area. Eventually, talk turns to mining and one of the men offers a description of what it's like to look for valuable opals. "Nothing could ever be truer than the old saying '**like looking for a needle in a haystack**'.[8] That's what it's like."

---

[7] **dwelling:** home or house
[8] **like looking for a needle in a haystack:** (expression) like trying to find something that is almost impossible to find

Predict

Think about the information that you have read to this point and answer the questions. Then check your answers on page 19.

1. How do the men's wives feel about the way of life in Coober Pedy?

2. What different opinions do they have about living there?

But if it's so difficult, why do the men look for opals instead of having other, more secure jobs? Another member of the team explains: "If we weren't opal mining, we could have quite good jobs. And if we'd had those for the last 20, 30 years, we would have been far better off financially." He then gives a big smile and explains further, "But we'd have missed out on all the fun!" His friend and fellow miner then adds, "[It's] the **lifestyle**."[9] After which the men conclude in agreement, "It's the lifestyle that keeps us here."

The lifestyle in Coober Pedy may be interesting for the men, but it's different for their wives. It's a hard life, they say. The families must often rely only on what the women earn to pay for life's necessities while the men dig. One of the wives explains: "Well, I personally think it's harder for the families. Because, I mean, day after day after day, and month after month, you don't know what's going on." She then goes on to say that there are financial concerns and stress that come with being in mining. "Basically you just know that there's nothing coming home," she explains, "or there's no opal coming home ... and like I said, I can't understand how [the opal miners] can do it day after day." And yet, despite the difficulties, people from 50 countries have come to this small town. Why do people give up their secure lives to come here?

---

[9]**lifestyle:** the manner in which one lives

Peter Rowe talks further about the attraction of mining for opals. "Within a mile of where we're sitting now, there could be millions of dollars," he says, and then corrects himself to emphasize that this is actually a fact, "There [are] millions of dollars." He then continues, "and there [are] stones that would knock your eye out. Gems that would be just **astronomical**.[10] And most of them never get seen. [They] never see the light of day."

Unfortunately, in Coober Pedy, these very valuable opals are rarely found and people often don't make their fortunes. Back at the mine, Neville Hyatt and his mining team are digging once again, hoping that today will be the day they find something. Eventually, they slow down the digging machines and go in using hand tools. The team slowly moves their tools across the stone walls of the tunnel, quietly searching and hoping for that one big stone.

---

[10]**astronomical:** describing an amount that is very large; here in price

At the end of a day that started with so much hope, Hyatt and his mining partners come up empty-handed—again. They didn't find that precious opal this time, but will they ever find the opal that will change their lives? Probably not. Mining is a **gamble**[11] and **the odds are against**[12] these miners. They may have hopes and dreams, and they may work hard, but the odds are that they won't find anything. They will almost certainly spend many years digging and earn hardly any money. The whole town knows that most people will not find enough opals to become rich. They know that they probably won't achieve their dream of **retiring**[13] with the money from their opal finds. So what makes people keep searching?

---

[11]**gamble:** something done at high risk with only a slight chance of success

[12]**the odds are against (something):** there is very little chance of something succeeding

[13]**retire:** stop working at a job for money

Peter Rowe describes why some people may become so intent on finding that one extremely valuable opal. It's a kind of madness, he says, that is created by the dream of finding that one elusive stone—and it does happen, sometimes. "Every now and again that one stone comes out," he explains, "You can never describe it to anyone. You can never get across to anybody what it looks like, because it not only represents something beautiful; it also represents the work that you yourself have put into finding that one stone." He then pauses and adds with a laugh, "[It's] totally **mad**[14] when you think about it."

---

[14]**mad:** crazy; not of sound mind

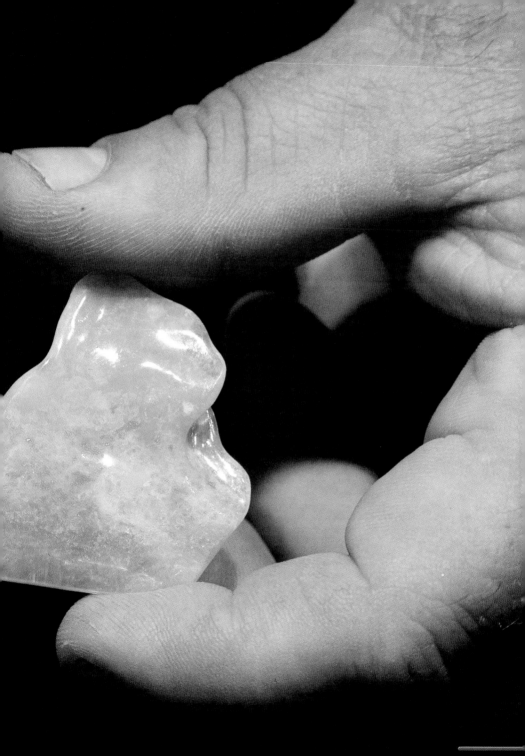

Perhaps this kind of 'opal madness' is how the people of Coober Pedy survive in the Australian outback. Perhaps it strengthens their ability to accept the thought that if they hadn't come, their lives probably could have been better. Maybe it helps them to deal with the heat, the dryness, and the days when they find only worthless opals. Perhaps this madness allows them to maintain their dreams so they can keep hoping for the day that they find one precious opal that changes their lives forever. It could be that opal madness gives the people of Coober Pedy the ability to endlessly search for a dream that sparkles, like a gem in the darkness.

What do you think?

1. Do you think that looking for opals really is a kind of madness?

2. Do you think the miners have done the right thing by leaving their secure life behind to look for opals in the outback?

3. Would you like to look for opals?

After You Read

1. Why did Peter Rowe move to Coober Pedy?
  A. to live in the Australian outback
  B. to become wealthy
  C. to mine for diamonds
  D. to research opals

2. Which of the following is true about opals in Australia?
  A. Coober Pedy is the opal capital of the world.
  B. The first opals were discovered in Australia in 1931.
  C. In Australia, opals can be found only in Coober Pedy.
  D. Australia provides 90 percent of the world's opals.

3. In the final sentence of paragraph 2 on page 8, to what does 'it's' refer?
  A. a piece of opal
  B. monetary value
  C. color
  D. fire

4. An appropriate heading for paragraph 2 on page 10 is:
  A. A Major Opal Discovery
  B. No Hope after Months of Digging
  C. Miners Keep Positive about Possibility
  D. Team Uneasy about Signs of Opals

5. Neville Hyatt believes that the process of finding opals is:
  A. ruled by chance
  B. aided by experience
  C. controlled by science
  D. assisted by research

6. Which of the following does NOT determine the price of an opal?
  A. stone cut
  B. color pattern
  C. stone shape
  D. stone thickness

7. Which word on page 16 means 'reside'?
    A. reach
    B. drop down
    C. live
    D. found

8. What is the main purpose of the miner's comment in paragraph 1 on page 19?
    A. to show that they are skilled professionals
    B. to explain their financial situation
    C. to demonstrate that mining is a secure job
    D. to show that they enjoy mining for opals

9. The mining lifestyle is difficult for wives because their husbands:
    A. are always working
    B. rarely, if ever, get paid
    C. often ask their wives to dig, too
    D. live far away from their families

10. What opinion does the writer express on page 23?
    A. Most miners will not achieve their goal.
    B. Mining is courageous work.
    C. Coober Pedy helps a lot of poor families.
    D. Miners like to be disappointed.

11. On page 24, 'it' in 'it does happen' refers to:
    A. acting mad
    B. having a dream
    C. finding a big opal
    D. describing a stone

12. What is the writer trying to explain on page 26?
    A. Miners in Coober Pedy are rejecting the outback life.
    B. Most miners will find an opal and leave Australia.
    C. The outback is the only place miners are understood.
    D. The dream of getting rich helps people survive a hard life.

Great Vacations, Inc.

Mine for Gems on Your Next Great Vacation!

Welcome to Gem-Mining Vacations!

On one of our gem-mining vacations, you'll have a chance to visit a variety of North Carolina gem mines that are open to the public. If you love gem stones or jewelry, it's the chance of a lifetime! Helpers at each mine will show you how to look for gems and where to find them right in the dirt. Some people collect gem stones for display in their homes. Others have their gems made into jewelry. Almost all of our mines have a jeweler on site so you can create a one-of-a-kind piece of jewelry just for you.

Fast Facts about Gem Mining

- Because of weather conditions, most gem mines in North Carolina are closed in the winter.

- A miner in Franklin County, North Carolina, once found a 2.5-pound ruby!

- At some mines you can actually find gold as well as gem stones in the soil.

- Gem stones can be made into buttons, tiny bottles, and other unusual objects.

Gem Stone Mining in North Carolina

The mines in North Carolina originally produced a mineral called 'corundum,' which is used in manufacturing processes. While mining this material, workers occasionally discovered rubies and sapphires, which are both expensive and rare gem stones. Unfortunately, there weren't enough of these stones to support a big gem-mining industry. However, there were enough to make things interesting, so the mines were opened to the public for hobby gem.

Equipment

Hand protection in the form of rubber gloves is a good idea. The dirt you'll search through is generally cold and wet. You'll also want sun protection for your skin and a hat to shade your face, especially in the summer. Plastic bags and other containers are useful for taking your gems home. Great Vacations will provide the rest.

Technique

Customers must pay for each bag of dirt (the first bag is free!). The dirt is then poured onto a small screen frame. Next, water is run over the screen to wash away the dirt while keeping any hidden gems on the screen. There are many things to look for while mining, but the main thing to watch for is color. A sparkle of red may be a ruby. A bright blue stone may be a sapphire. A good-sized stone of any type is a valuable find!

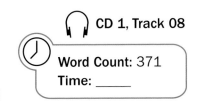

CD 1, Track 08

Word Count: 371
Time: _____

Vocabulary List

astronomical (20)
bounce out (7)
dwelling (16)
elusive (7, 24)
fist-sized (13)
fortune (13, 20)
gamble (23)
gem (2, 3, 7, 8, 11, 20, 26)
intensity (2, 8)
landscape (3, 4)
lifestyle (17, 19)
like looking for a needle in a haystack (16)
mad(ness) (24, 26, 27)
mine (3, 4, 7, 10, 11, 13, 14, 16, 19, 20, 23, 27)
monetary (8)
opal (2, 3, 4, 7, 8, 10, 11, 13, 14, 16, 19, 20, 23, 24, 26, 27)
precious (2, 3, 7, 23, 26)
retire (23)
sparkle (2, 8, 26)
stake a claim (3, 10)
the odds are against (23)
the outback (3, 4, 26, 27)
tunnel (3, 4, 14, 20)